How to p

TENNIS

a step·by·step guide

Series editor:
Mike Shaw

Technical consultant:
Brian Blincoe SNASC
LTA Panel Tutor

JARROLD

Other sports covered in this series are:

AMERICAN FOOTBALL
BADMINTON
BASKETBALL
BOWLS
COARSE FISHING
CRICKET
CROQUET
GET FIT FOR SPORT
GOLF
HOCKEY
SAILING A DINGHY
SNOOKER
SOCCER
SQUASH
SWIMMING
TABLE TENNIS
WINDSURFING

How to play TENNIS
ISBN 0-7117-0420-1

Illustrations by Malcolm Ryan

First published 1989
Reprinted 1995

Designed and produced by
Parke Sutton Limited, Norwich
for Jarrold Publishing, Norwich
Printed in Great Britain 2/95

Contents

Introduction

Tennis is a sociable, energetic game that is good exercise and, above all, fun to play. It can be played at any age – either as singles or doubles – and between men and women, boys and girls of all ages and standards. Singles is traditionally seen as the more energetic game, although a hard match of doubles can be just as tiring!

Tennis is continually growing in popularity in this country. There are thousands of tennis courts in parks, clubs and sports centres throughout the United Kingdom which can be rented for very reasonable fees by the hour. The local city council amenities department can usually put you in touch with your nearest public courts. Alternatively, you can find a tennis club in most towns which you can usually join for an annual membership fee. The extra costs of joining should usually guarantee well-maintained courts, a regular source of opponents, expert tuition as well as some social facilities.

Although tennis is increasingly played indoors, it is essentially an outdoor game associated in most people's minds with the drama of Wimbledon and long summer afternoons. However, modern outdoor all-weather surfaces, floodlights and the rapidly growing number of excellent indoor courts now make all-year-round tennis a possibility for most players.

A closely contested match can take a couple of hours or more and is a great way for two or four people to get some good exercise on a summer's afternoon – or at any other time of year!

The Court

Tennis was originally played on grass but nowadays is also played on cement, clay, asphalt, artificial grass, carpet and other surfaces.

The court's surface will affect the style of play: rough surfaces like asphalt and shale are slow, encouraging defensive play, whereas smooth surfaces including well-maintained grass are fast and encourage attacking play.

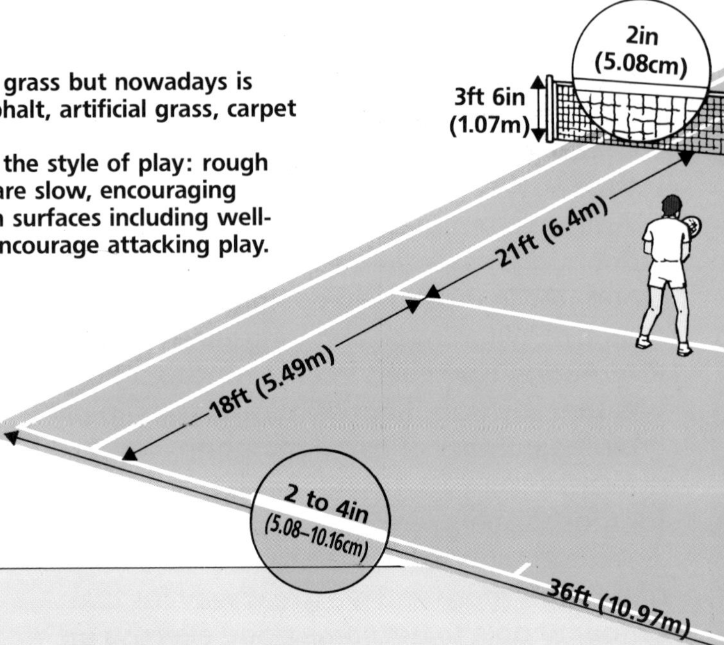

The Net

Before play wind the net up, using the handle in the post, until taut, then check that the centre of the net is the correct height (3ft (0.91m)). The net is usually wound down between play to take the strain off the posts. It should also be turned over to prevent fraying in the wind.

The two lines down the side of the court marking the singles and doubles courts are traditionally referred to as the 'tramlines'.

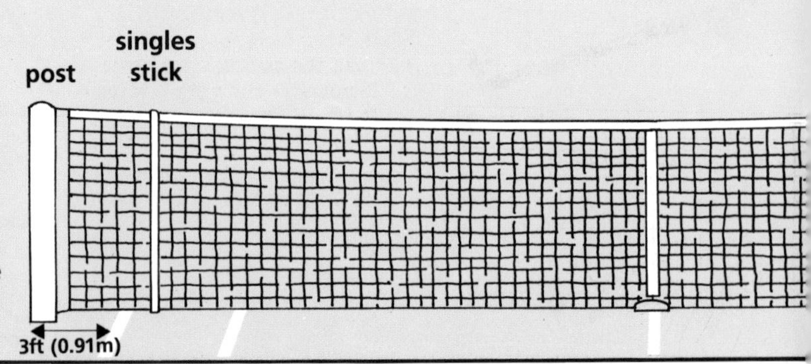

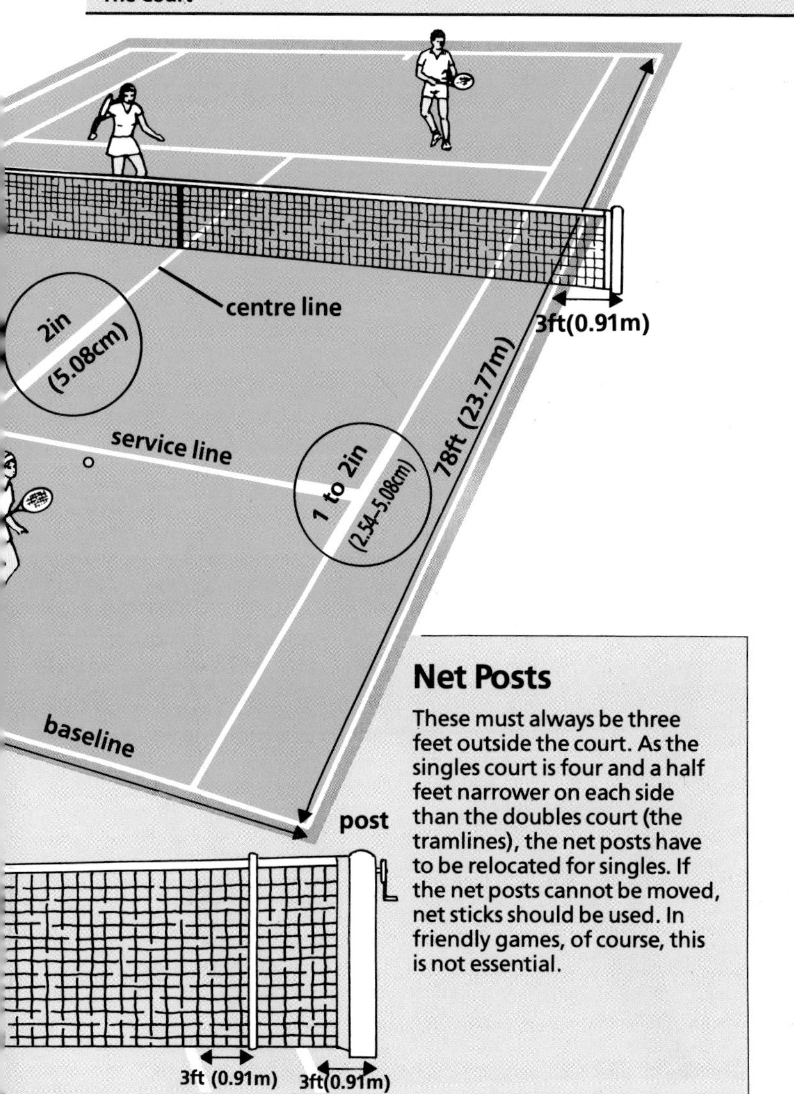

Net Posts

These must always be three feet outside the court. As the singles court is four and a half feet narrower on each side than the doubles court (the tramlines), the net posts have to be relocated for singles. If the net posts cannot be moved, net sticks should be used. In friendly games, of course, this is not essential.

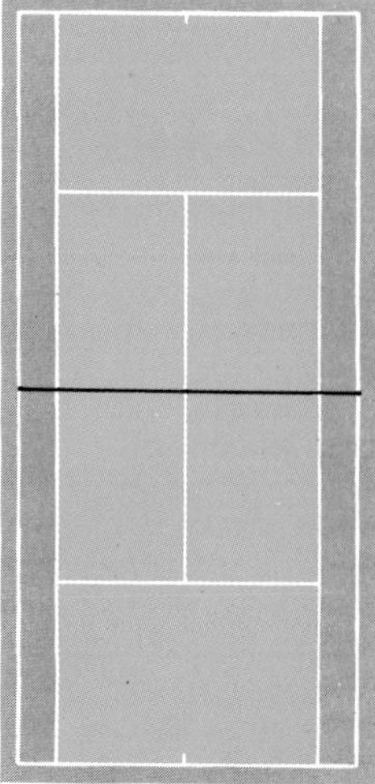

Doubles Court

Equipment

The only equipment you must have is a racket and balls.

Tennis Rackets

Traditional tennis rackets were made of laminated wood and strung with gut, but today many other materials such as steel, aluminium and carbon fibre are used for frames, and nylon for the strings.

Gut is more responsive than nylon but breaks more frequently and is affected by moisture, becoming slack. Your local sports shop should have a stringing service which you will need from time to time.

Following the introduction of Short Tennis for young beginners there is now a complete range of strung rackets from 19in (48.26cm) to full size available at sports shops. So whatever their age and size, a player can select a racket of suitable weight, length and handle size.

Hold the racket close to the end of the handle. Check that the grip size is comfortable. If it feels clumsy or heavy you might need a lighter racket or a smaller grip – ask for advice from a sports shop or professional coach.

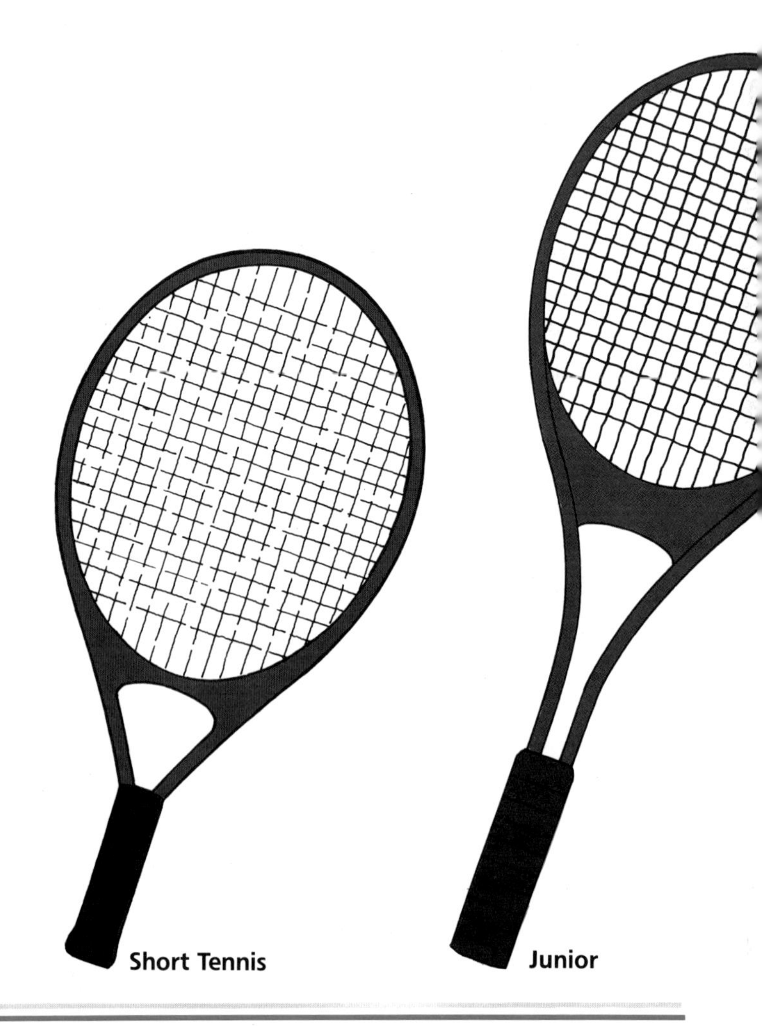

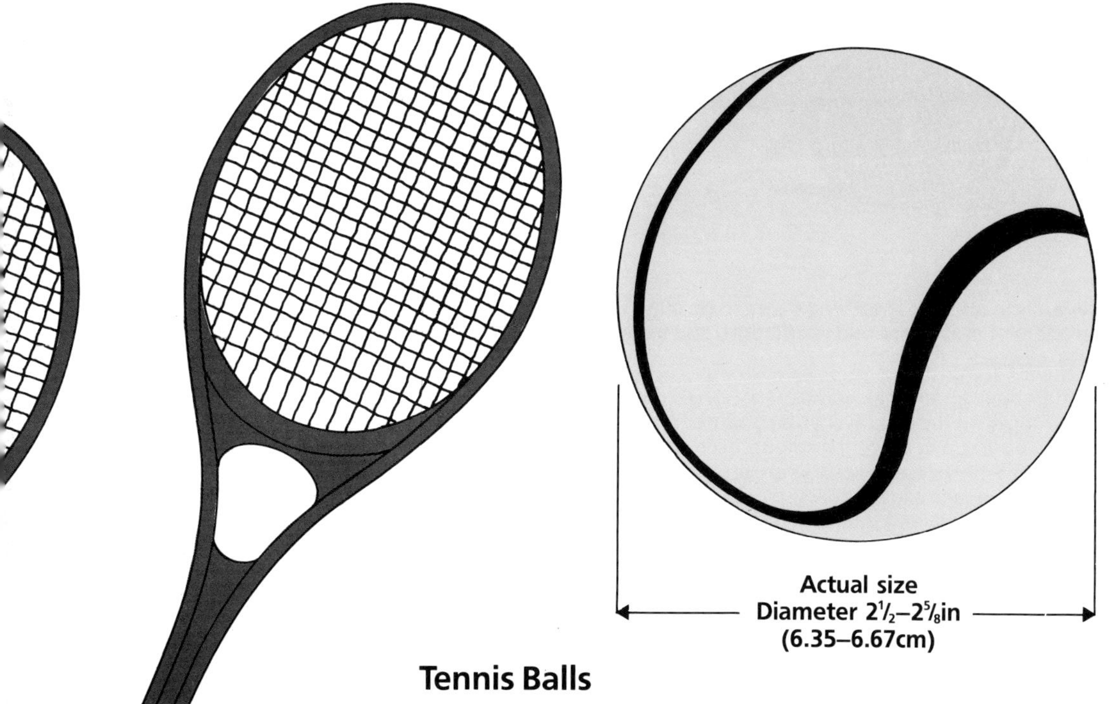

Adult

Tennis Balls

Tennis balls are made of rubber and covered in either wool (the knap) or a man-made imitation fibre. Despite the decorative 'seam', they are actually seamless. Traditionally balls were white, but yellow balls are now more popular. Balls with worn knap are harder to control than new ones.

Balls are pressurised so that when dropped onto concrete from 100in (2.54m) they bounce at least 53in (1.34m), but not more than 58in (1.48m). For normal recreational play pressureless balls may be used which last longer and are more consistent.

As with rackets the evolution of Short Tennis and the transition to the full-scale game has seen the range of balls expanded by the introduction of slower-moving, lower-bouncing foam and low compression balls for young beginners.

Clothing

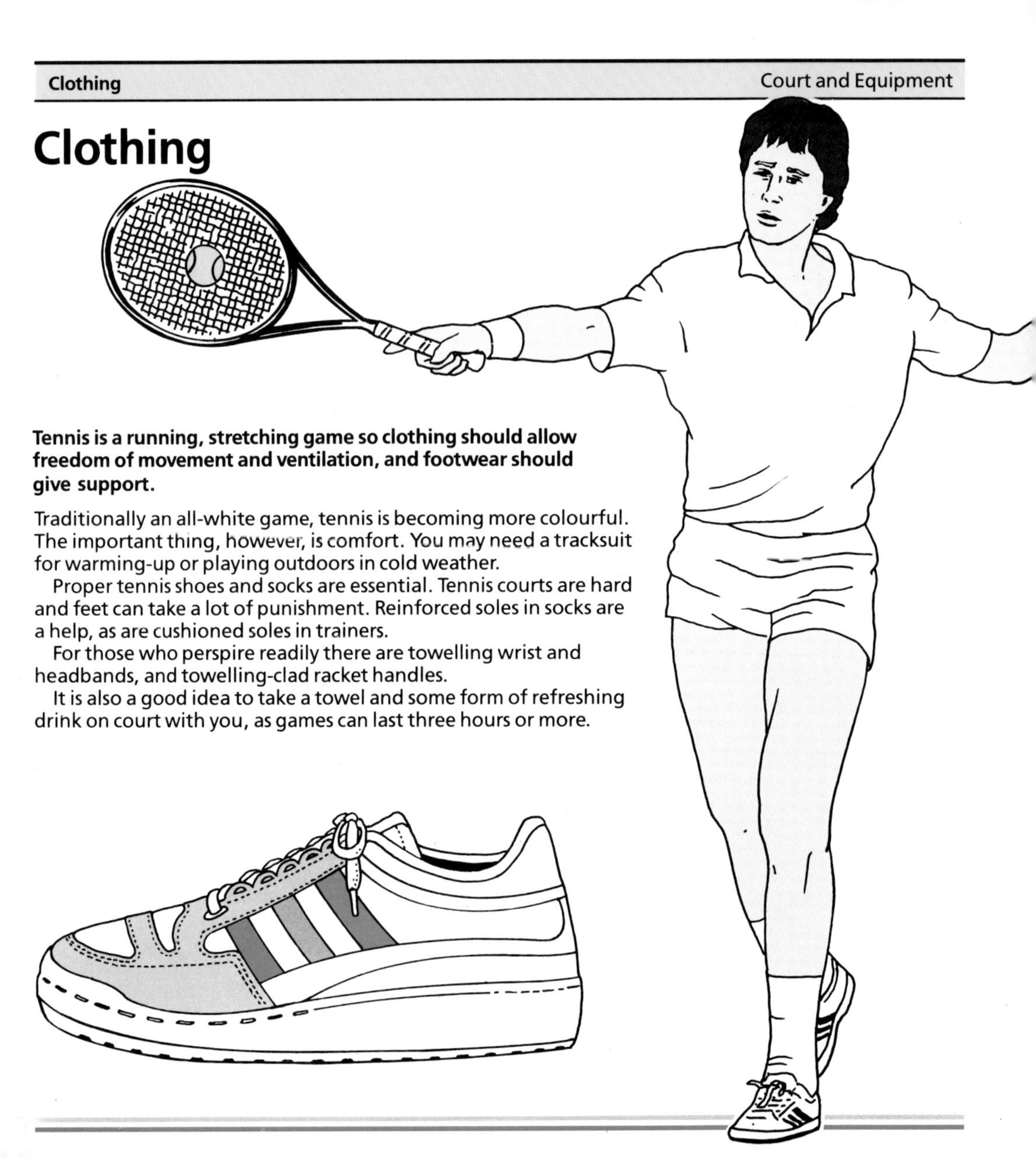

Tennis is a running, stretching game so clothing should allow freedom of movement and ventilation, and footwear should give support.

Traditionally an all-white game, tennis is becoming more colourful. The important thing, however, is comfort. You may need a tracksuit for warming-up or playing outdoors in cold weather.

Proper tennis shoes and socks are essential. Tennis courts are hard and feet can take a lot of punishment. Reinforced soles in socks are a help, as are cushioned soles in trainers.

For those who perspire readily there are towelling wrist and headbands, and towelling-clad racket handles.

It is also a good idea to take a towel and some form of refreshing drink on court with you, as games can last three hours or more.

The Toss

The game begins with the toss of a coin or, if your racket includes 'rough and smooth stringing', you can spin to decide who will serve first and the choice of end from which the players will start.

Whoever wins the toss may make one of these decisions or pass the decision. Whoever makes the first decision leaves the second decision to the other player.

Thus there are four possible outcomes if you win the toss:

1	**Choose to serve.**	**Opponent chooses ends.**
2	**Choose not to serve.**	**Opponent serves and chooses ends.**
3	**Choose ends.**	**Opponent chooses who serves.**
4	**Choose not to choose.**	**Opponent chooses 1, 2 or 3.**

Order of Serving

Singles

In singles, players take it in turns to serve. A player serves for an entire game from one end. The first serve is always taken from the right-hand side, the second from the left, the third from the right and so on.

At the end of the first game the players change ends. Thereafter they change at the end of every odd-numbered game for the rest of the match. In effect this means you serve one game from one end and your next service game from the other.

Doubles

In doubles the rules on serving and changing ends are the same as for singles but the players serve in rotation. Each side decides which player shall serve first and then maintains this sequence throughout the set. So if Team 1 (A and B) is playing Team 2 (C and D) and Team 1 decides A shall serve first and Team 2 that D shall serve first the order of services would run as follows:

Game 1: A serves. Change ends.
Game 2: D serves.
Game 3: B serves. Change ends.
Game 4: C serves.
Game 5: A serves again. Change ends – and so on.

In effect this means that players always serve from the same end and for this reason it is permitted for a team to change their order of service at the beginning of each set but not during a set.

At the beginning of each set the teams must decide which player is to receive on the right-hand side and which on the left-hand side. Once decided a player receiving serve on the right-hand side will continue to do so throughout the set. It is, however, permitted for a team to change receiving sides as well as the order of service at the beginning of each set if they wish.

Serving and Receiving Courts

Singles

In singles, the blue area of the court is not used at all.

When A serves to B it must be into one of the two service courts. If A serves from the right-hand side the ball must land in the orange service court. If A serves from the left-hand side the ball must land in the yellow service court.

When B returns the ball, however, it can land anywhere in the red court. And when A returns the ball to B it can land anywhere in the purple court.

Doubles

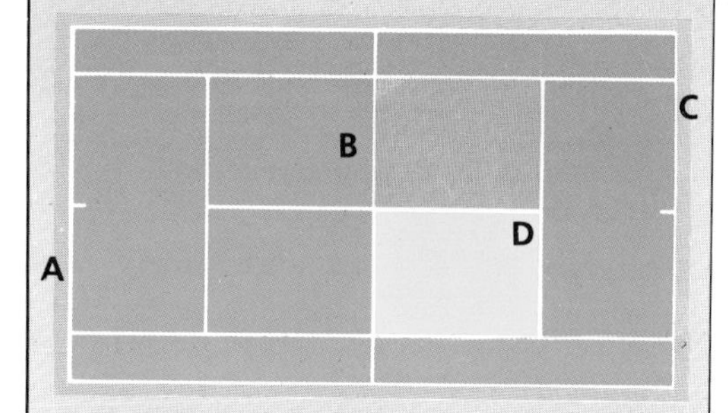

In doubles the service courts are exactly the same as for singles. If A is serving to C from the right-hand side the ball must land in the orange area. If A is serving from the left-hand side the ball must land in the yellow service court.

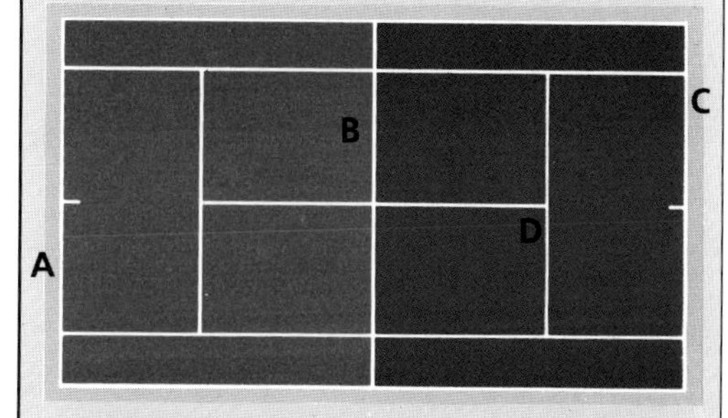

When C returns the ball, however, it can land anywhere in the red court. And when A or B returns the ball it can land anywhere in the purple court.

Scoring

Game . . .

The simple objective of tennis is to get the ball into your opponent's court. Failure to do so loses you a point.

How many points do you need to win a game?

The answer is simple. Four points win a game, providing you have a two points' lead. Otherwise the game continues until one player does have a clear two points' lead. The names for the points derive from the quarters of a clock face.

0	love	1	fifteen
2	thirty	3	forty

3 – 0 would be described as forty-love, 1 – 2 is fifteen-thirty, etc.

The server's score is always called first. So if the server has no points and the opponent three, the score would be love-forty.

Once you get to forty you can win the game with your next point. So 40 – love, 40 – 15, 40 – 30 are all game-winning positions. 40 – 40, however, is not because even if you win the next point you would not have a two point lead.

If both players get to forty the previous method of scoring is abandoned altogether, and the score becomes 'Deuce' which means 'evens'. If a point is scored after Deuce, then the player gains an 'Advantage', and if the next point is also won, then that player goes two ahead and is thus the winner. If, however, the other player wins the next point then the scores are again even, and so it is back to Deuce.

AT THE END OF A GAME:

The service goes to the opposing player or team.

If it is an odd-numbered game, the players change ends.

AT THE BEGINNING OF THE NEXT GAME:

The server first serves from the right-hand service area.

Set . . .

How many games do you need to win a set?

Six, providing you have a two-game lead. So 6 – 0, 6 – 1, 6 – 2, 6 – 3, 6 – 4 all make a set, but 6 – 5 does not. If the score progresses from 6 – 5 to 7 – 5 the leading player wins that set. If, however, the score goes to 6 – 6 a tie-breaker may be played. In games played for fun you can choose either to play a tie-breaker or to play on until one player gains a two-game lead.

Before the introduction of tie-breakers, games often progressed to 21 – 19 and more.

and Match

Matches are played to the best of three or sometimes five sets. Best of three or five means the number of sets to be played is limited to three or five. The player who wins the most sets is the winner. Ladies' singles and mixed and ladies' doubles are played to the best of three sets; men's singles and men's doubles may be played to the best of five.

Most 'informal games' are played to the best of three.

In matches played to the best of three, for example, if one player is 2 – 0 up the match is over, even though three games have not been played. Even if the other player was to win the third game and makes the score 2 – 1 the match would remain lost.

Tie-Break

Tie-breakers are usually played when a set reaches 6 – 6 but are not always used in a deciding set. The player who was due to serve the next game serves the first point of the tie-break. The service changes after the first point and each odd-numbered point thereafter. Servers serve from the right then the left as usual. Players change ends after each six points played.

How many points do you need to win a tie-break?

Seven, but you must be two points clear. So you can win 7 – 0, 7 – 1, 7 – 2, 7 – 3, 7 – 4, 7 – 5 but not 7 – 6, only 8 – 6 and so on.

AFTER A TIE-BREAK:

The winner of the tie-break wins the set by seven games to six.

The players change ends.

The player who served the first point in the tie-break becomes the receiver in the first game of the next set.

Serving

The server must place the ball in the air with one hand and strike it with the racket in the other before it hits the ground. The ball must travel over the net and land directly in the service court diagonally opposite. The server has two attempts at a service before losing the point, and must alternate sides for serving each point.

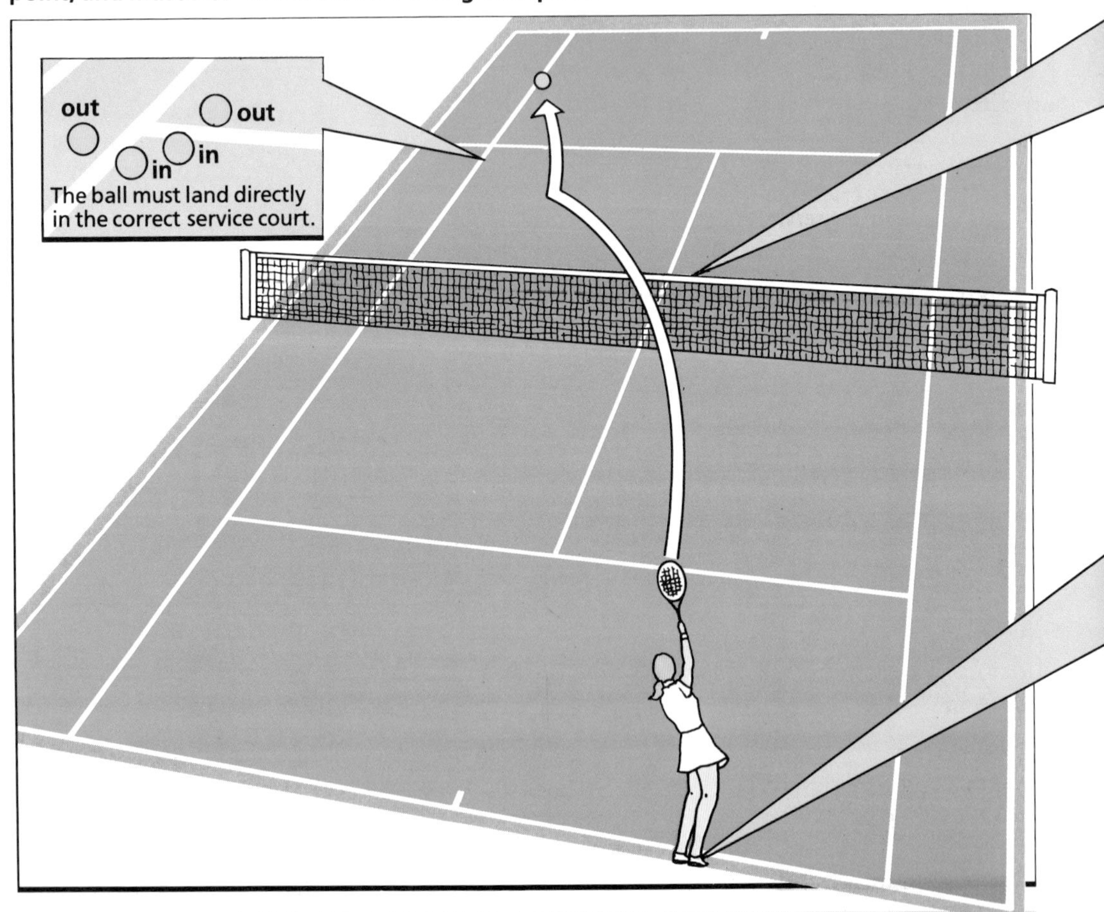

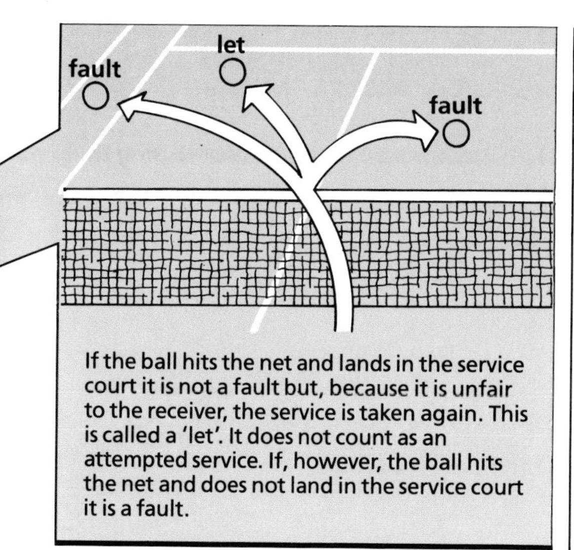

If the ball hits the net and lands in the service court it is not a fault but, because it is unfair to the receiver, the service is taken again. This is called a 'let'. It does not count as an attempted service. If, however, the ball hits the net and does not land in the service court it is a fault.

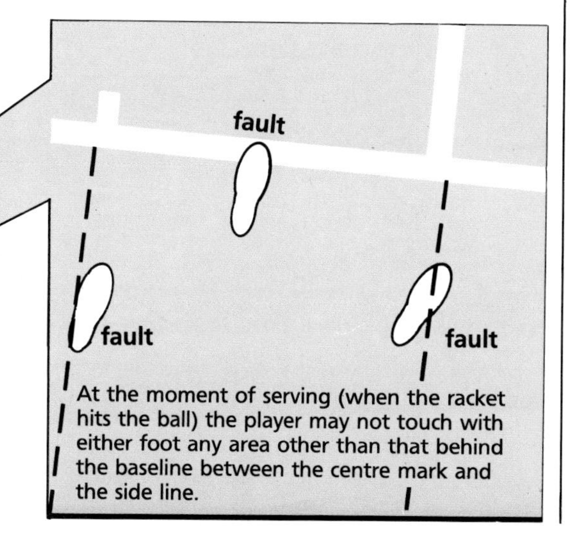

At the moment of serving (when the racket hits the ball) the player may not touch with either foot any area other than that behind the baseline between the centre mark and the side line.

A Point

The ball may only bounce once on your side of the net before it must be hit back into the other player's court. This continues until you or the other player loses the point. After each point the server changes sides for the next service.

You lose a point if:

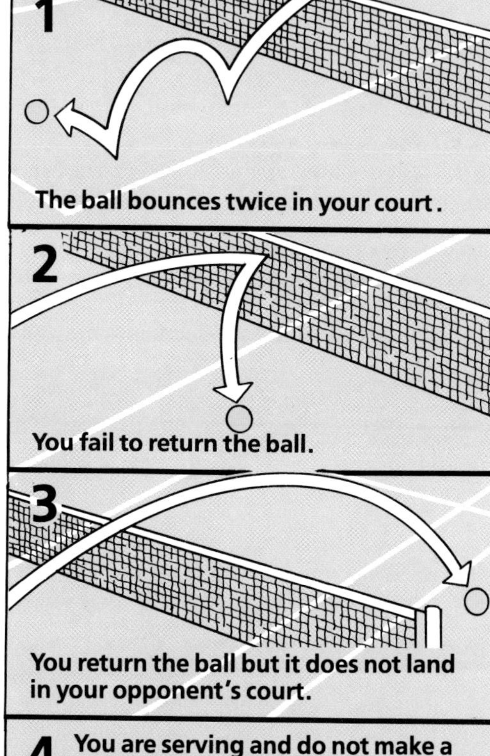

1 The ball bounces twice in your court.

2 You fail to return the ball.

3 You return the ball but it does not land in your opponent's court.

4 You are serving and do not make a good service after two attempts.

Faults

There are several other ways in which a point or one service attempt can be lost:

1 Foot fault

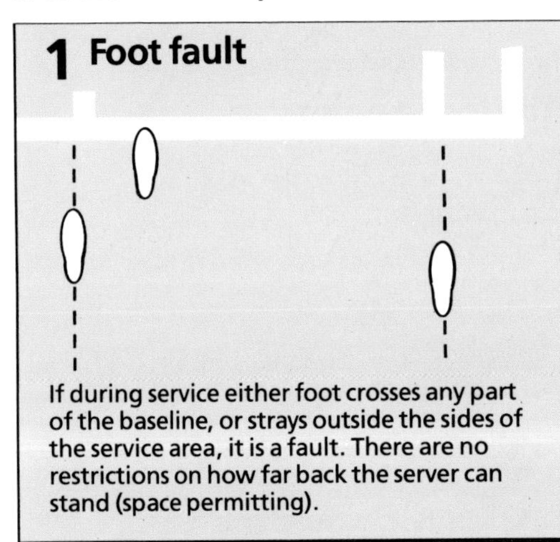

If during service either foot crosses any part of the baseline, or strays outside the sides of the service area, it is a fault. There are no restrictions on how far back the server can stand (space permitting).

2 Foot movement

If the server should run or walk while serving it is a fault. Small movements such as jumps, are allowed. Discretion is required in this area.

3 Missing the ball

If during service the server misses the ball it is a fault. If, however, no attempt is made to play the ball it is a let.

4 Volleying a serve

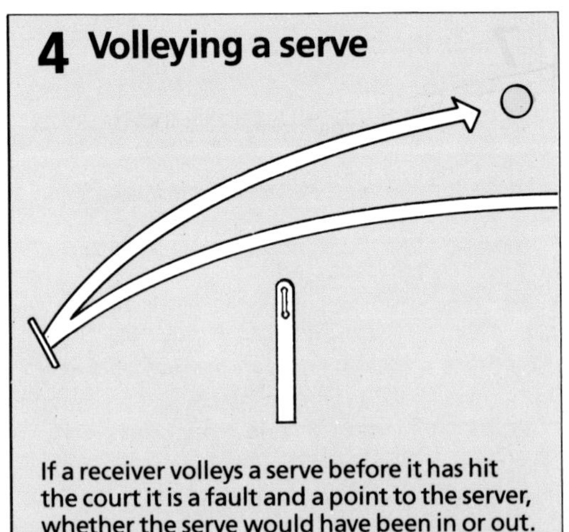

If a receiver volleys a serve before it has hit the court it is a fault and a point to the server, whether the serve would have been in or out.

5 Double hit

If a player hits a ball twice before it crosses the net or 'carries' the ball on the racket, or both players in a doubles team hit a ball consecutively, it is a fault.

6 Throwing the racket

If a player throws the racket at a ball and hits it, even if the ball goes over the net, it is a fault.

7 Ball obstruction

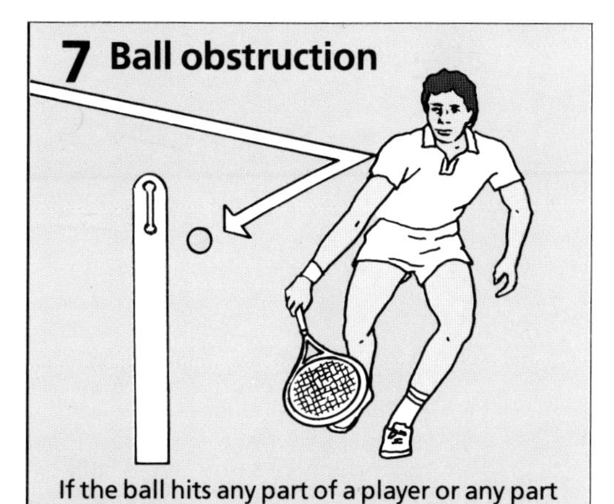

If the ball hits any part of a player or any part of a player's clothing except the racket, it is a fault.

8 Playing over the net

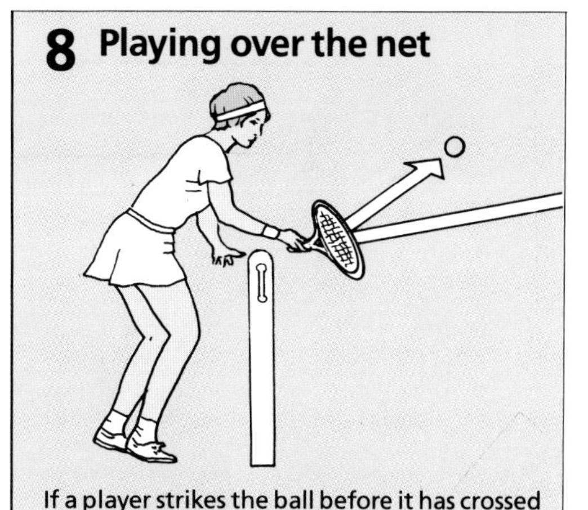

If a player strikes the ball before it has crossed the net it is a fault.

9 Touching the net or opponent's court

If a player touches the net or any part of the opponent's court with either the body, clothing or the racket it is a fault.

10 Hitting an opponent's partner

In doubles, if the serve is good and is obstructed either before or after the bounce by the receiver's partner, it is a fault to the receiver.

11 Hitting a partner

If it is your serve in doubles, and the ball hits your partner, your partner's clothing or racket, it is a fault, even if the serve goes in.

12 Hitting permanent fixtures

If you hit any permanent fixture apart from the net or posts – stands, umpire's chair, court walls, ceiling etc. – before the ball bounces in your opponent's court it is a fault. If a fixture is hit after the ball has bounced, however, it is your opponent who loses the point.

Non Faults

1 Hitting the net

If you hit any part of the net – posts, centre strap, net band or wire – and the ball carries on into court it is not a fault and play continues – although if you are serving, you play a let.

2 Serving out of turn

If a service is made out of turn it is not a fault. The point(s) stand, but the rightful server takes over from the correct position with a first serve. If the game is completed before the mistake is discovered, it stands.

3 Hitting temporary fixtures

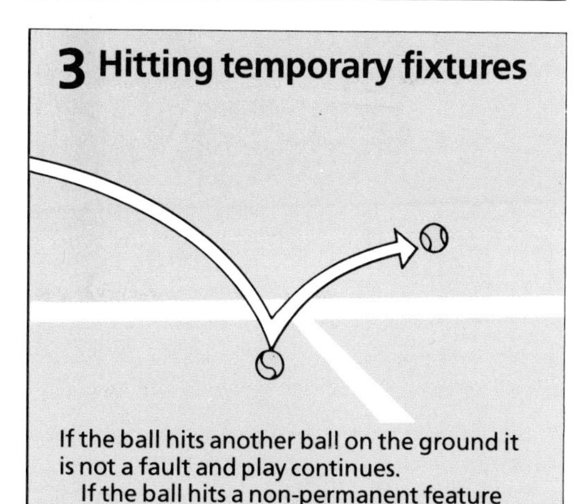

If the ball hits another ball on the ground it is not a fault and play continues.

If the ball hits a non-permanent feature such as a pigeon or a player on an adjacent court, you should play a let.

4 Serving from the wrong end or side

Again the point(s) stand but the server must move to the correct end or side. If a whole game has been played it stands.

5 Serving before the opponent is ready

If a server serves before the receiver is ready a let is played. If however the receiver makes any attempt to play the shot it stands.

6 Damaged ball

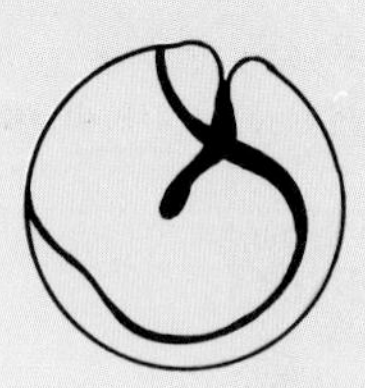

If a ball becomes damaged during play, then play a let.

7 Round the posts

If a ball is played very wide and the receiver takes the ball well out of court, and returns it round the posts but into court, it is a good return even if it returns below the level of the net.

8 Bounce or blow back

If, due to a lot of backspin or wind, a ball bounces in your court and is blown or spins back over the net, you can hit it providing you do not touch the net or your opponent's court. If you do not hit it, or hit it after it has bounced in your opponent's court, you will lose the point for failing to return the ball.

The Grip

The diagrams below refer to a right-handed player. Whether players hit their backhands with one or two hands is a matter of personal preference.

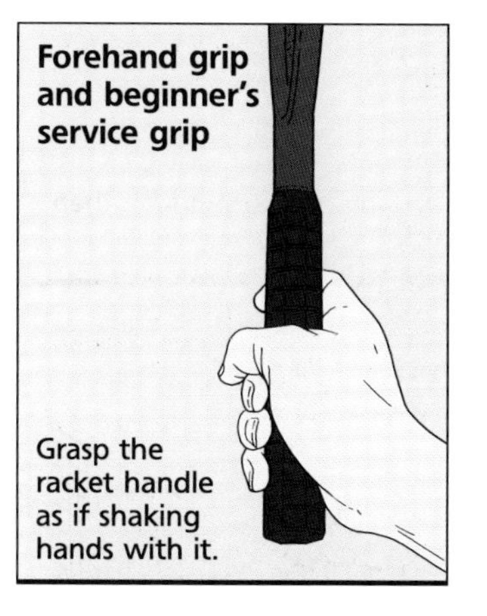

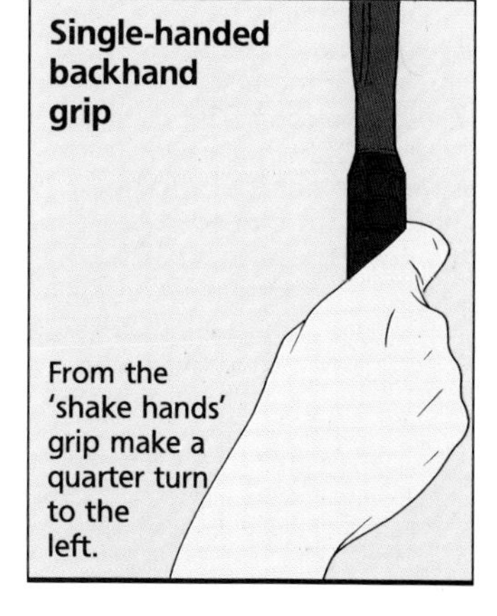

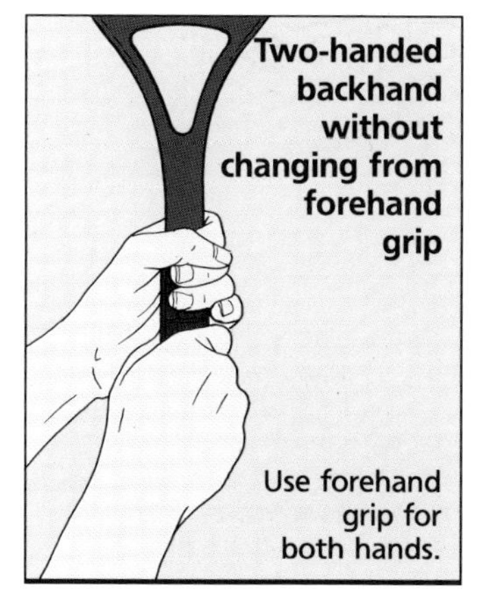

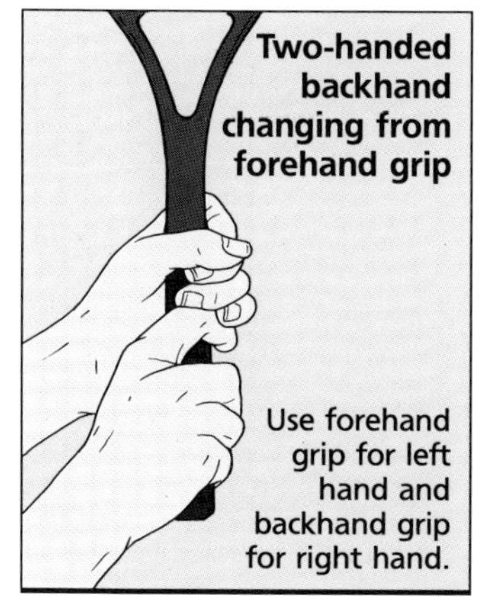

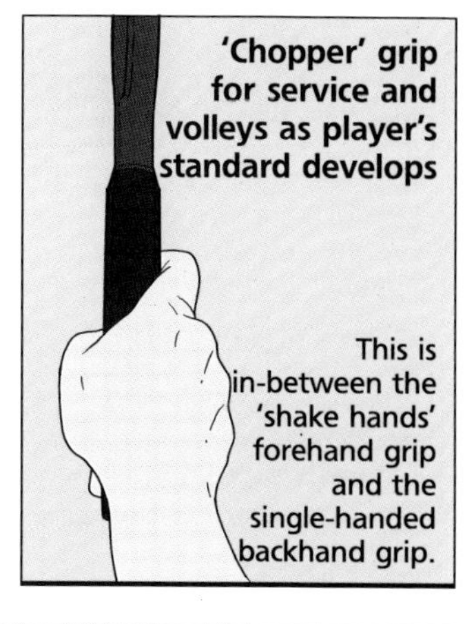

The Service

Very young players start by serving underarm, which is a legal service provided the ball is hit before it bounces, but the transition to the overhead serve should be made early on. Start by standing in the service area and throw the ball overarm into the service court. Get used to how hard the ball needs to be thrown to get it in and how much height is needed to clear the net. Throwing a ball is exactly the same as serving a ball. Try it. Throw a ball into the service court, then place one into the air in front of you and throw it in by hitting it with the racket held with the other hand.

Useful tips

- **Always keep your eye on the ball.**
- **Place the ball in the air so that it is about twelve inches in front of your front foot. Try this a few times. Let the ball fall to the ground and see where it lands.**
- **Place the ball a few inches higher than you can reach with your racket when really stretching, and hit it as it comes down.**
- **Get the serve in, speed will come later.**

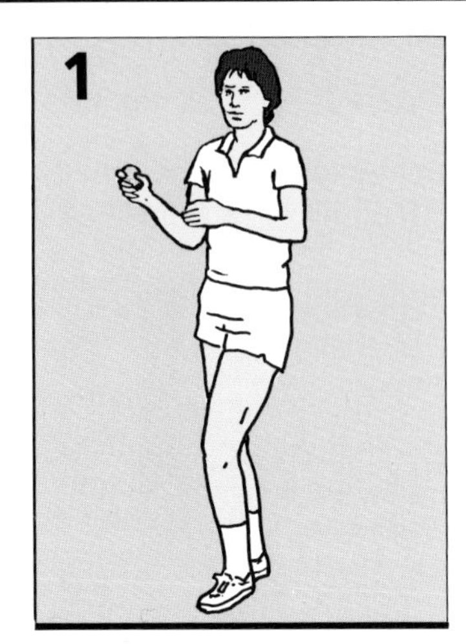

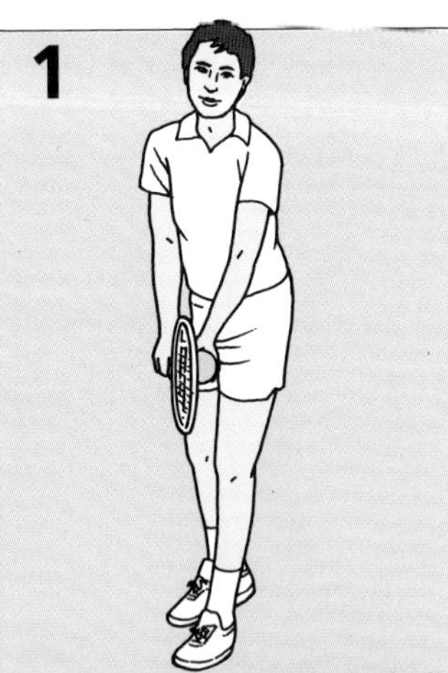

Touch your racket with the ball hand – it helps coordination. Show the racket to the service court just as you would a ball.

Move both arms together. Use the whole arm to place the ball in the air, not the wrist. Keep your eyes on the ball.

3

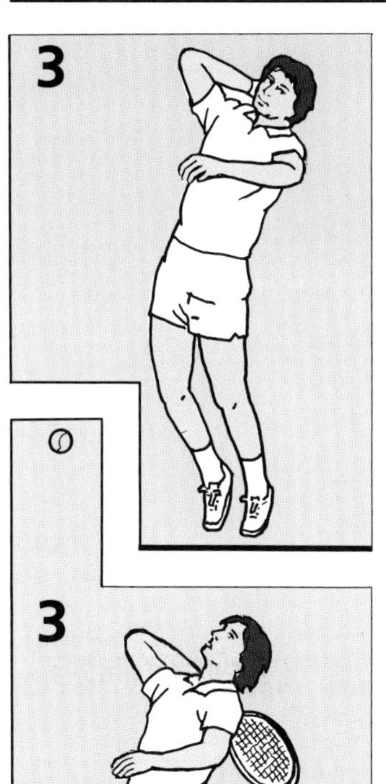

3

The ball goes up, the racket comes back; weight moves from the back foot.

4

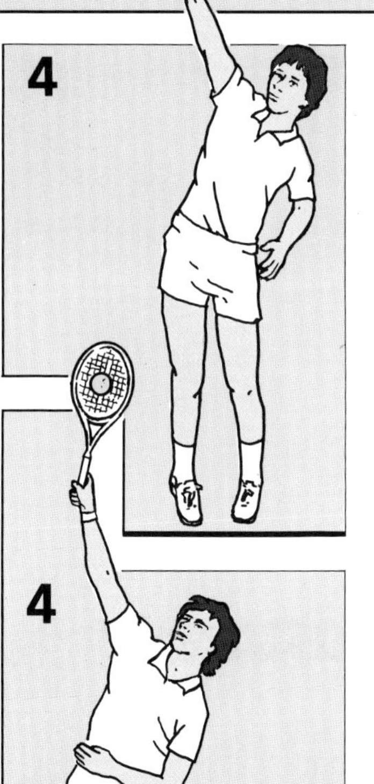

4

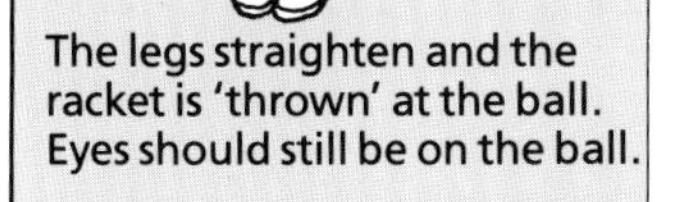

The legs straighten and the racket is 'thrown' at the ball. Eyes should still be on the ball.

5

5

Let the racket shoulder follow through, then the leg will come forward and help you into the court.

Returning the Service

Receiving stance

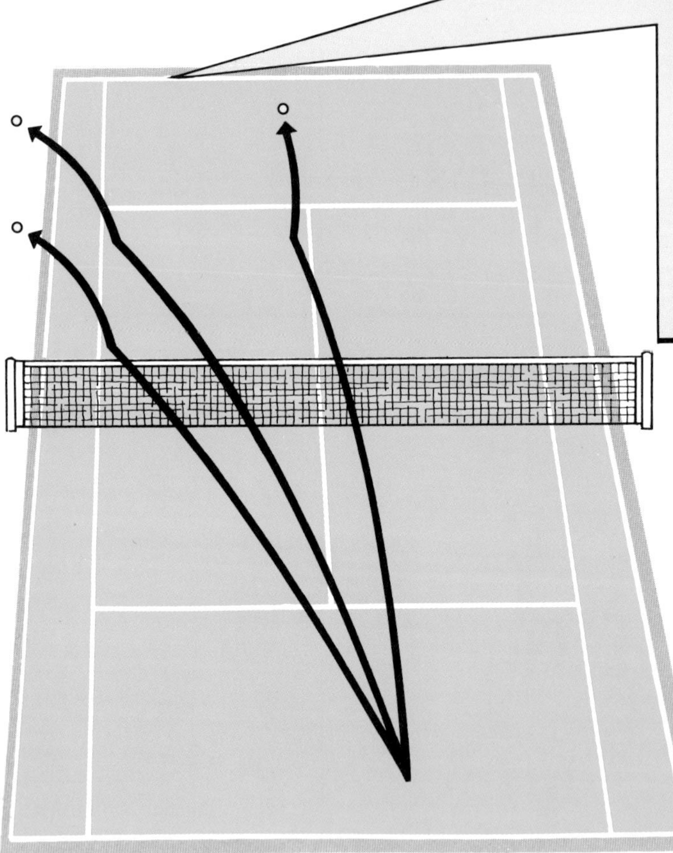

Despite the rather small size of the service court, good players using various spins can send the service ball in a variety of directions. Adopt a position sufficiently far back to give yourself time to see the ball, react and get to it, but not so far that you are left stranded out of court after your return.

Most players serve more deliberately on a second serve so you can usually come forward a little if their first serve has gone out.

Adopt an alert stance. A good serve comes very quickly, and you will have to move rapidly either to left or right, so keep your racket forward ready for either and stay on the balls of your feet.

– **And watch the ball!**

Positioning during Rallies

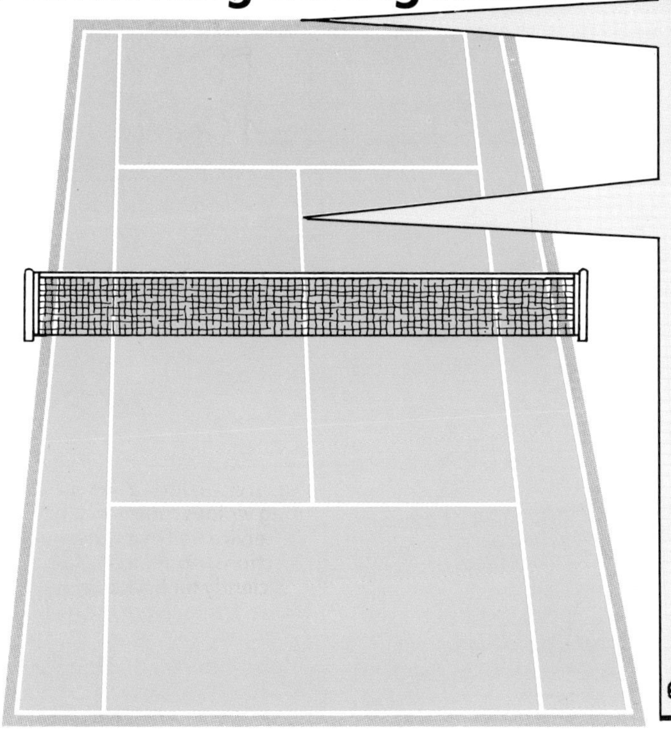

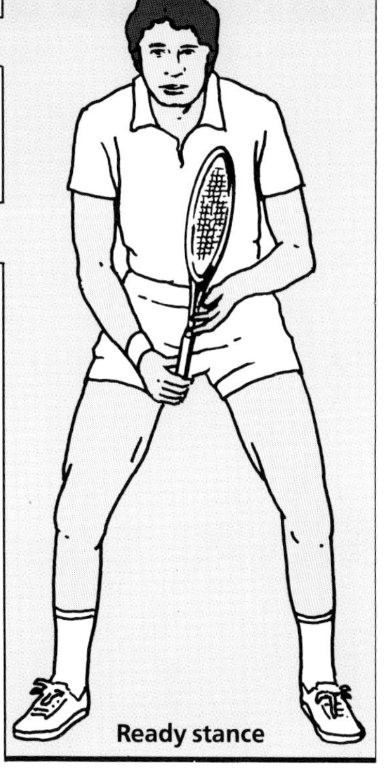

Ready stance

Before demonstrating the basic strokes it is important to understand that you are defending your court and attacking your opponent's.

Your positioning should be either just behind the baseline, if you are playing from the back of the court, or at a reasonable distance from the net if volleying (– reach out and touch the net with your racket and take one large pace back).

Keep in the alert stance, on the balls of the feet. Top players, you will notice, often do a little gig to keep their bodies in suspension. Remember you may have to travel left or right, forward or back. When you see the shot coming *move!*. Being swift on your feet is important in tennis. Get your feet into a position where you can play the shot comfortably, then run again.

Beginners often stop to admire their returns. Remember, hitting the ball is only the first part of the stroke, getting back on position is the second. – **And always watch the ball!**

The Forehand Drive

This is the easiest and most frequently used shot in tennis. It is an underarm swing using the racket.

1

Start from the ready position.

2

Turn sideways as you take the racket back.

3

Prepare to play the ball between knee and waist height as it is falling from the top of the bounce.

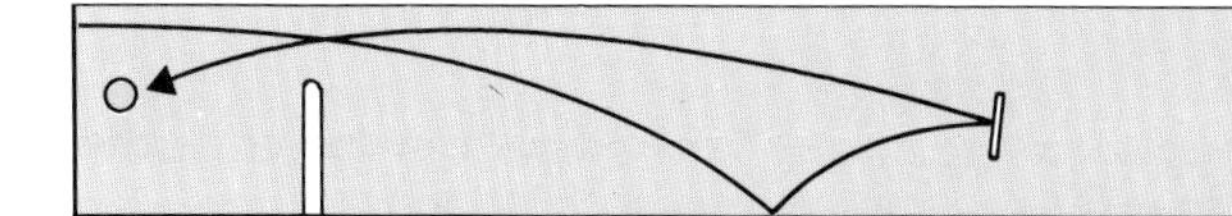

4

Keep your wrist firm throughout the swing.

5

Transfer your weight forwards as you swing the racket to hit the ball out to the side but in front of you. Watch the ball onto the strings.

6

Keep a good follow-through, then recover to the ready position.

The Backhand Drive

This is a hard shot for beginners. Most people learn to 'throw' and 'swipe', but they do not learn to do it backhand, so strength and co-ordination are usually both lacking.

Apart from that, it is basically the same shot as the forehand.

1

Move so you are lined up with the ball. Start from the ready position

2

Turn your shoulders as you take the racket back. Watch the ball, and decide where to put it.

3

Prepare to play the ball between knee and waist height as it is falling from the top of the bounce.

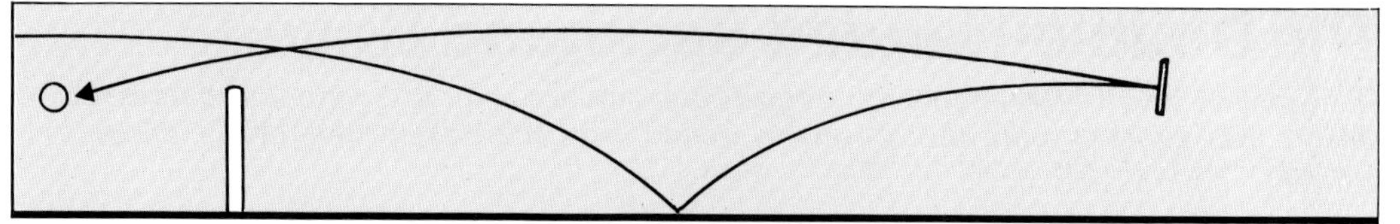

Keep your wrist firm throughout the swing.

Transfer your weight forward as you swing the racket with a feeling of 'lift'. Hit the ball out to the side but just in front of you. Watch the ball onto the strings.

Keep a good follow-through, then recover to the ready position.

The Double-Handed Backhand Drive

Some players find the two-handed shot gives them more power and control. Positioning and balance are, however, more critical and the second hand may be removed for the follow through.

1

Move so you are lined up with the ball. Start from the ready position.

2

Turn your shoulders as you take the racket back. Watch the ball, and decide where to put it.

3

Prepare to play the ball between knee and waist height as it is falling from the top of the bounce.

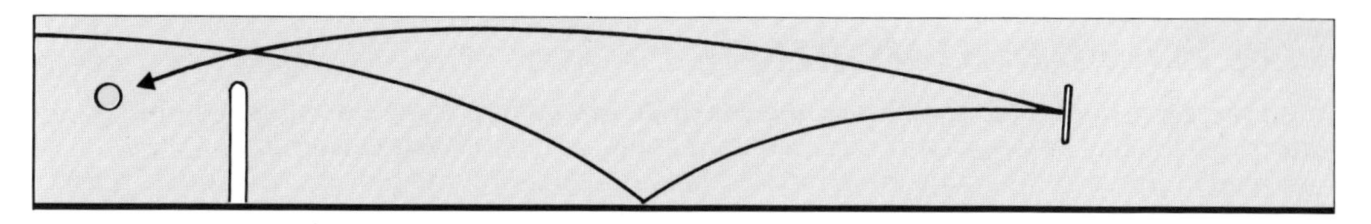

4

Keep your wrist firm throughout the swing.

5

Transfer your weight forward as you swing the racket with a feeling of 'lift'. Hit the ball out to the side but just in front of you. Watch the ball onto the strings.

6

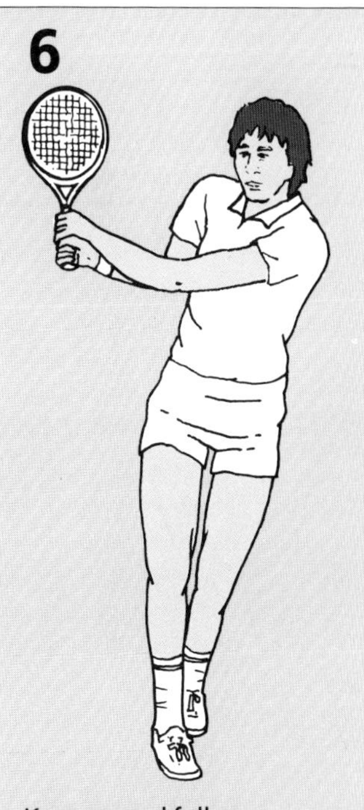

Keep a good follow-through, then recover to the ready position.

The Forehand Volley

If the serve can be likened to a throw and the drive to a swing, then the volley is a punch. You attack the ball before it can bounce in your court, as if you were 'catching' it.

As you improve at the game, then rather than just 'catching' the ball you will 'push' it and eventually 'punch' it back over the net using its own momentum on the racket to redirect it. Only volley close to the net.

1

From the ready position punch or block your racket towards the ball.

2

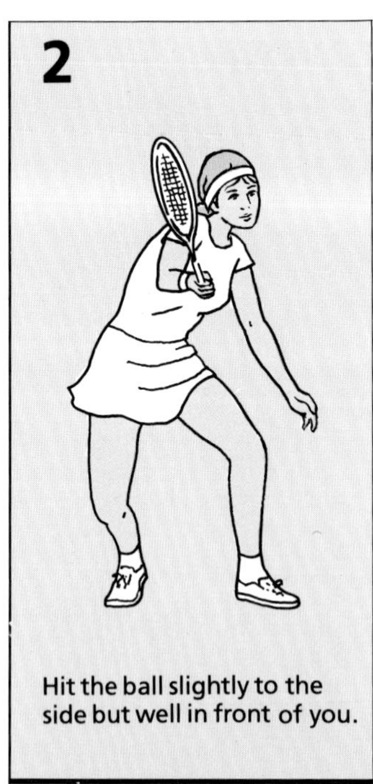

Hit the ball slightly to the side but well in front of you.

3

Keep the punch short. Recover to ready position.

The Backhand Volley

Rather than changing your grip for the backhand volley, try using a continental (chopper) grip for all volleys – no grip change is then necessary.

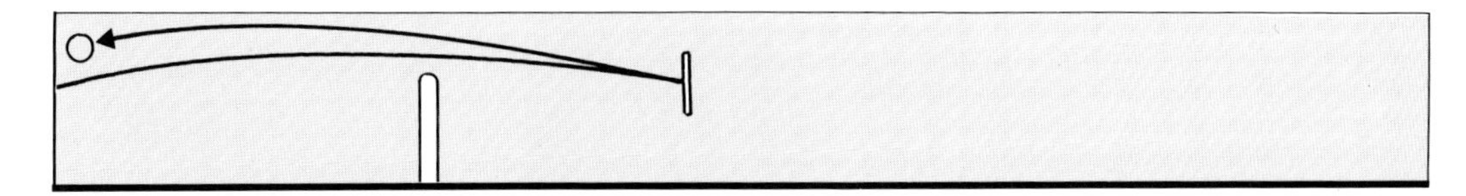

1

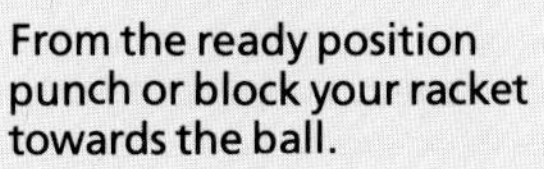

From the ready position punch or block your racket towards the ball.

2

Hit the ball slightly to the side but well in front of you.

3

Keep the punch short. Recover to ready position.

The Smash

The action used to smash the ball is very similar to the service action. It is used for returning high shots from your opponent. If your opponent has played a very high shot you may decide to let it bounce first and smash the bounce. There is little point in trying to smash until you have mastered serving.

1

Keep your eyes on the ball. Position yourself under the ball.

2

Decide where you are aiming the smash. Open the arms. Weight onto the back foot.

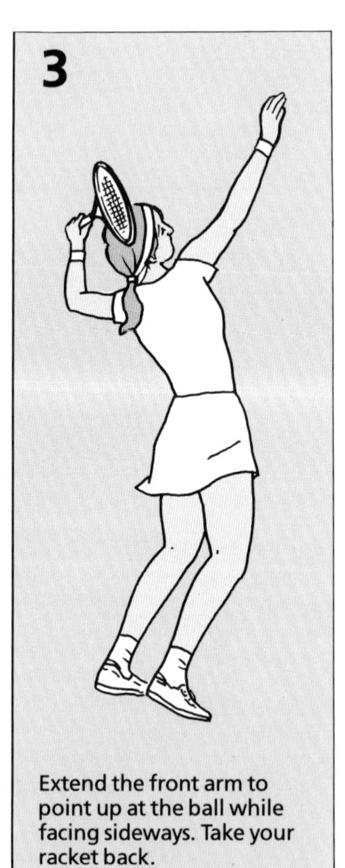

3

Extend the front arm to point up at the ball while facing sideways. Take your racket back.

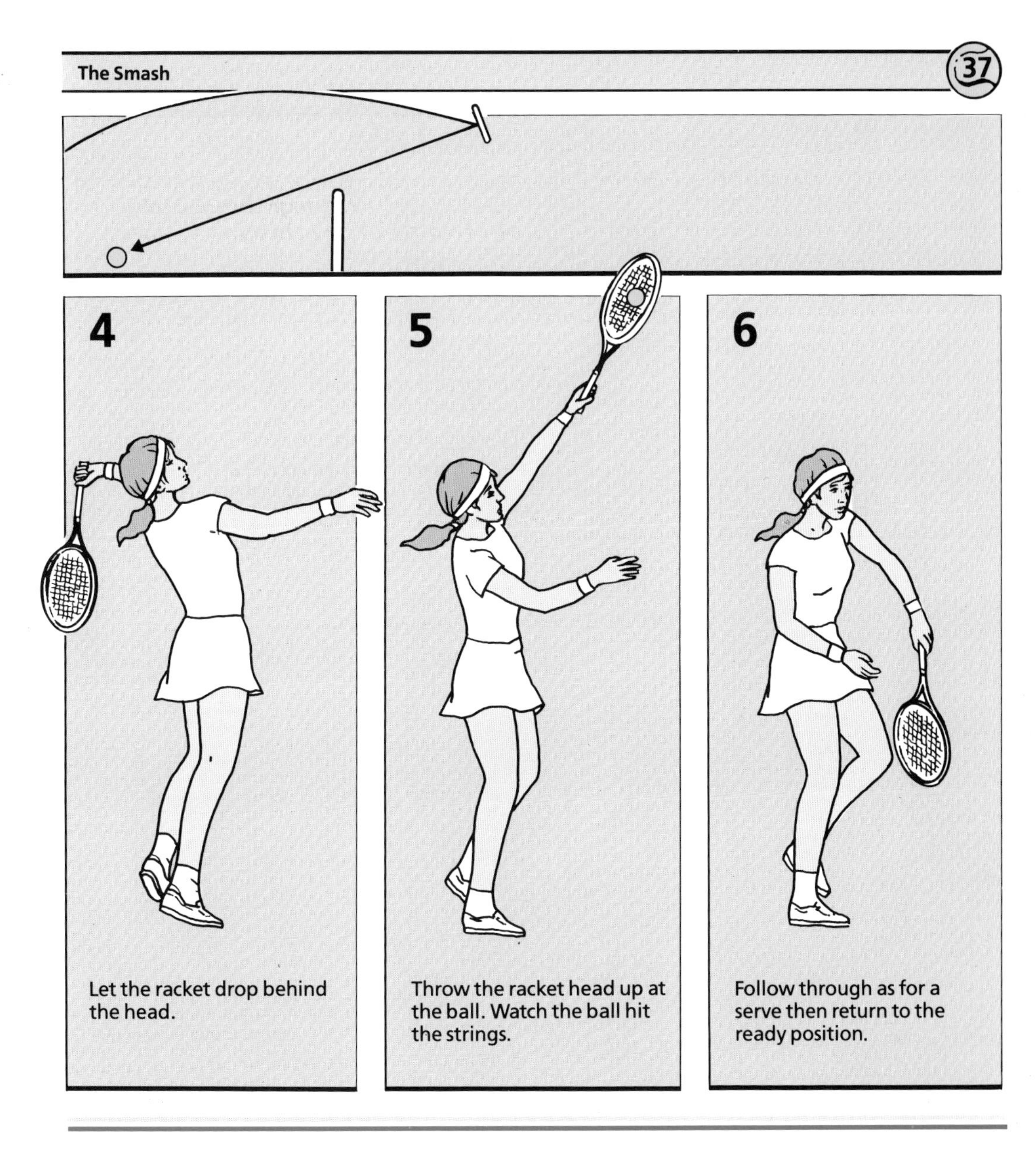

4

Let the racket drop behind the head.

5

Throw the racket head up at the ball. Watch the ball hit the strings.

6

Follow through as for a serve then return to the ready position.

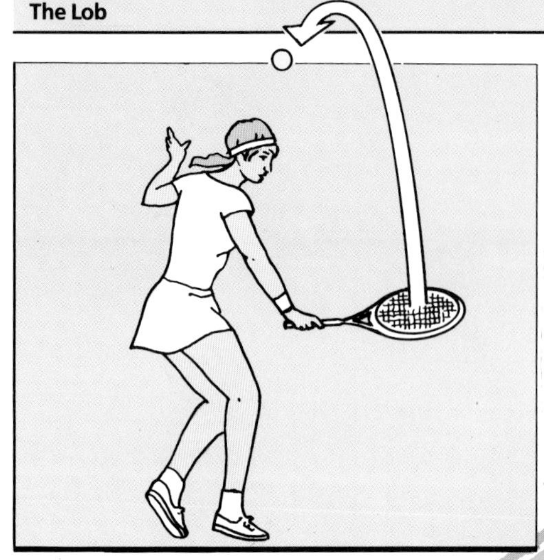

The Lob

This shot is played both in attack and defence. The object is to play a ball over your opponent and out of their reach.

Attacking lob

If your opponent is close to the net and plays a weak shot you can lob over their head, possibly to win the rally. Lob high enough to just clear their outstretched racket. Lobs hit with top spin can be very effective as they drop sharply and hurry away after bouncing.

Defensive lob

If your opponent sends you far out of position you can lob them to gain time to recover. In this case, play the ball as high and as deep as possible.

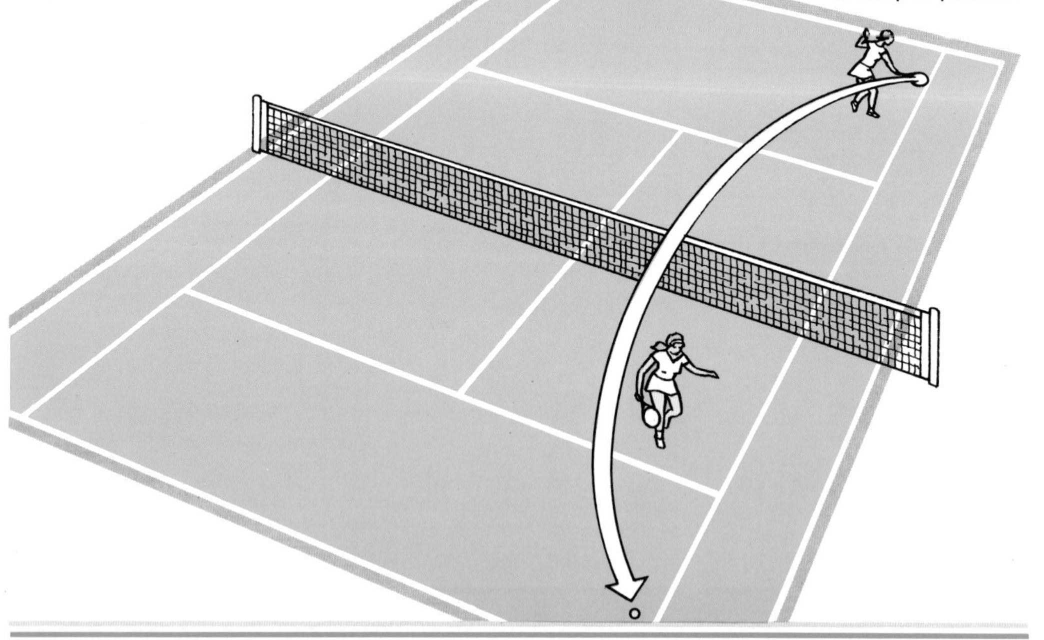

The Dropshot

This shot is played with backspin to make the ball bounce in your opponent's court as near to the net as possible. It is played either as a drive or volley and should be disguised until the last moment.

The object of the shot is to confuse the opponent and force a badly executed return, or to so wrong foot the player as to be able to score an outright winner.

The Spin

To hit a ball with spin – instead of hitting it squarely with the racket face – you hit it with the racket face angled. The object of spin is to cause the ball to deviate from its normal path after the bounce. Spin also affects the flight of the ball.

Topspin

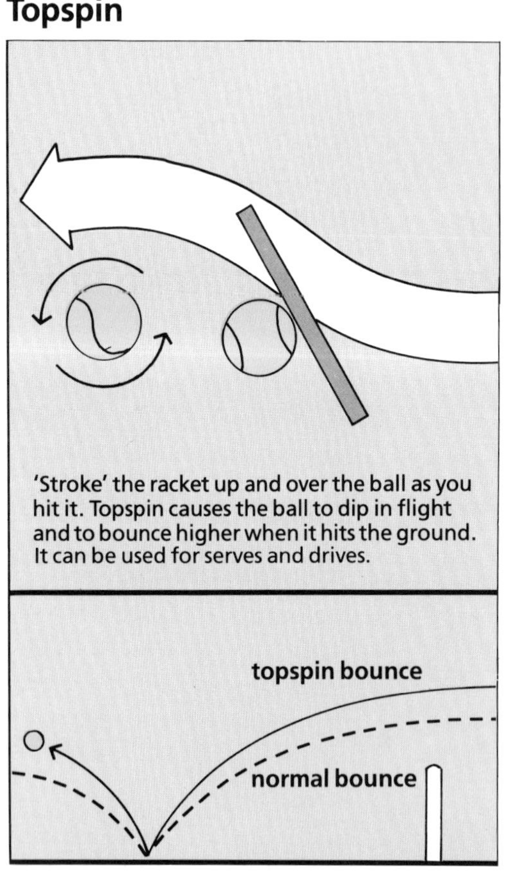

'Stroke' the racket up and over the ball as you hit it. Topspin causes the ball to dip in flight and to bounce higher when it hits the ground. It can be used for serves and drives.

Slice or underspin drive

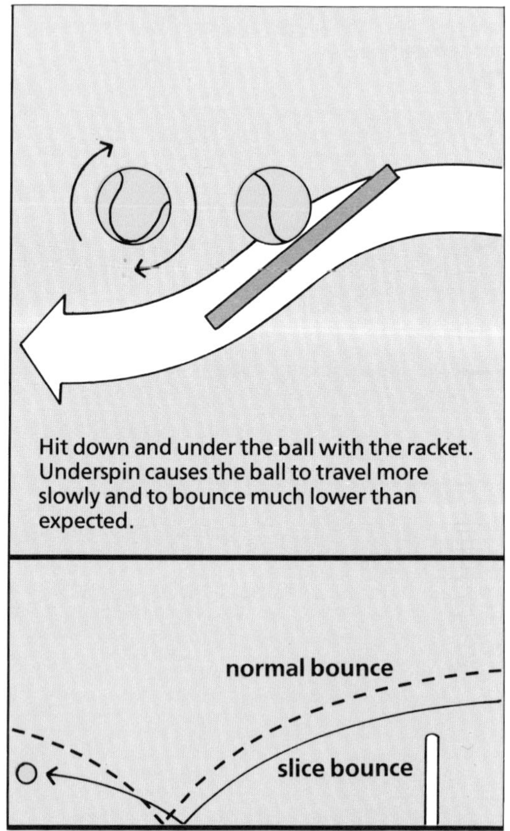

Hit down and under the ball with the racket. Underspin causes the ball to travel more slowly and to bounce much lower than expected.

Slice or sidespin service

'Slice' around the side of the ball with racket as you hit it Sidespin causes the ball to swerve out to the right or left (according to which side has been hit) both in flight and particularly after the bounce. The sliced service will thus make the ball either veer out of court or into the receiver's body after the bounce.

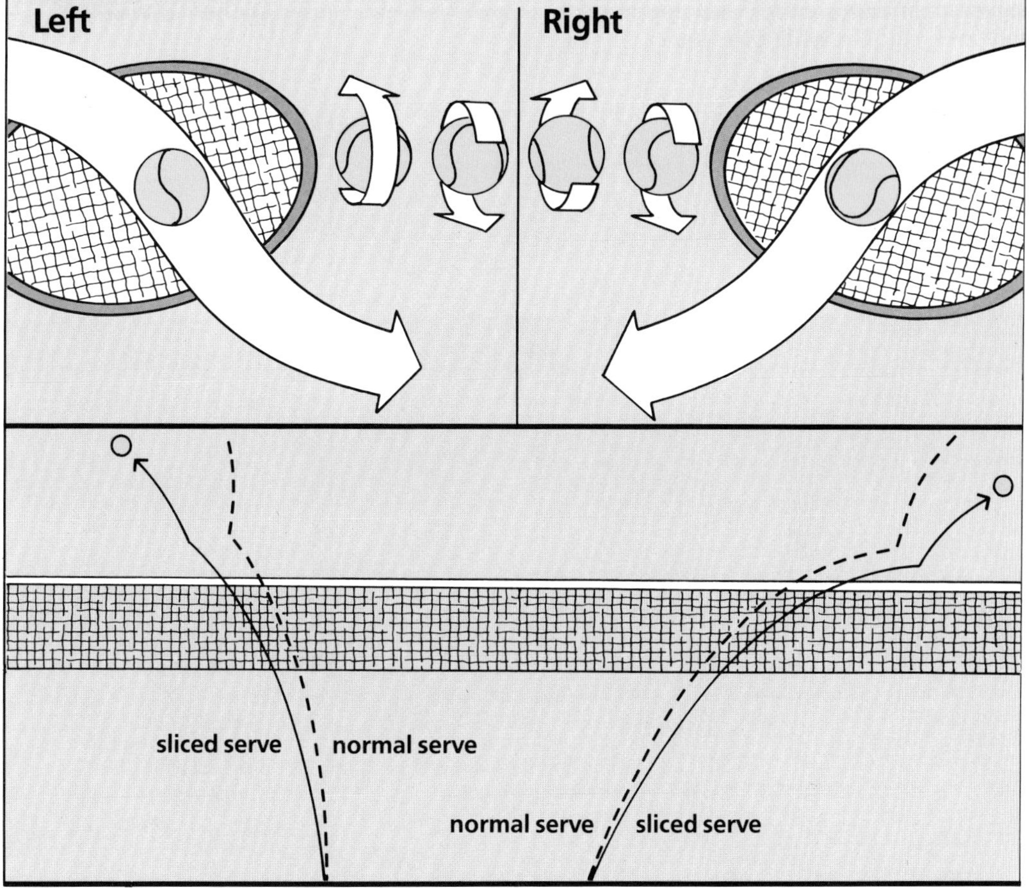

Left

Right

sliced serve

normal serve

normal serve

sliced serve

Singles Tactics

The basic strategy is to try and force your opponent to play a bad return or better still to fail to return the ball at all. This can be achieved in a number of ways. Try and place the ball in the most difficult spot for your opponent to return. Also, note your opponent's weakest shot and play to it whenever you can.

Opponent at the net

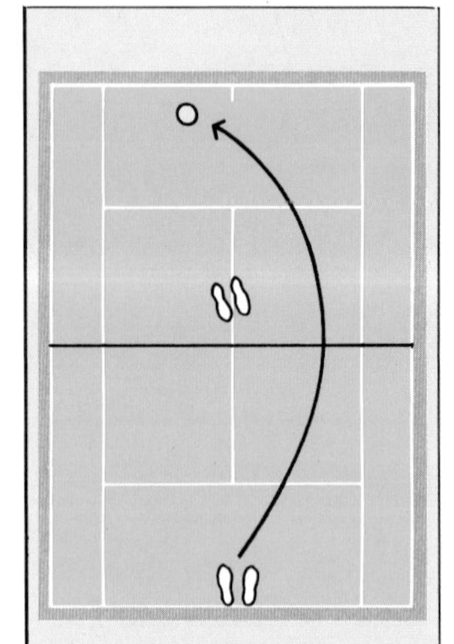

If you are at the back of the court and your opponent is at the net, try a lob – but remember it must be deep and high or it will be smashed.

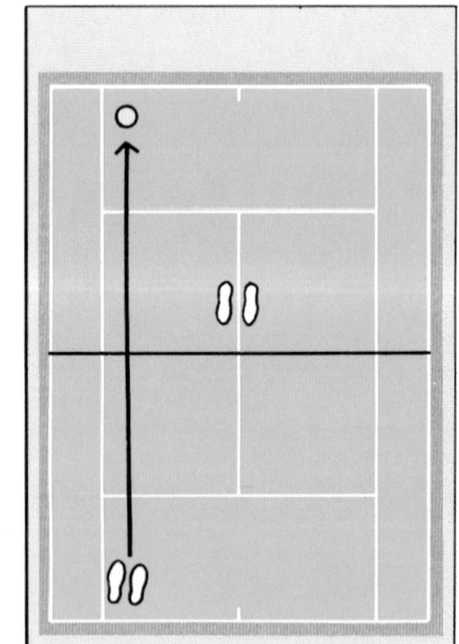

If you have been forced wide, turn it to your advantage with a down-the-line passing shot. Keep it deep and above all keep it in play. This shot is even more effective from a very wide position.

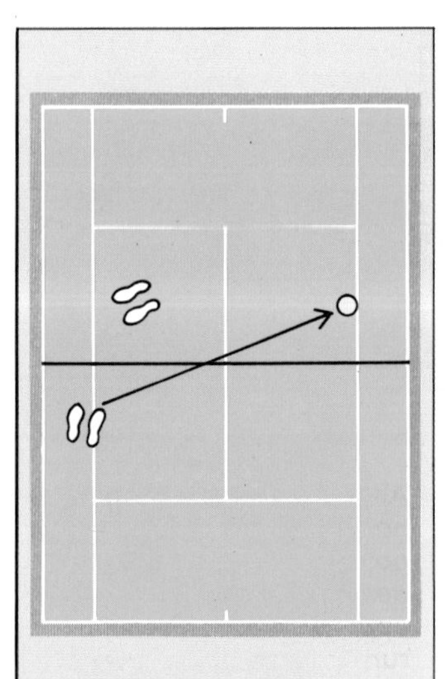

If your opponent is moving to cover the down-the-line shot you might attempt a low, angled cross-court shot although this requires excellent control and balance.

Opponent at the baseline

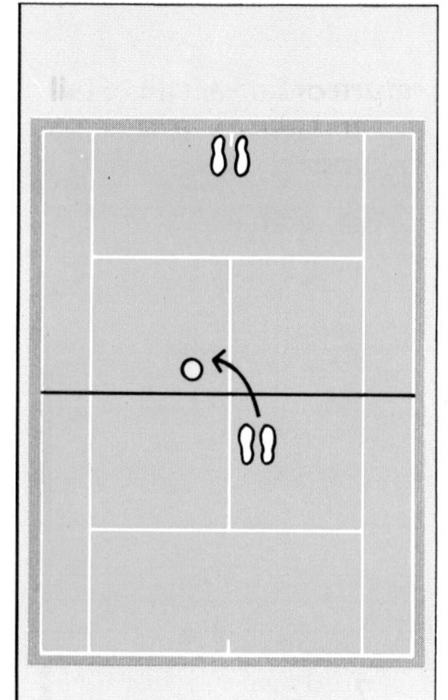

Although this shot should not be over used, the occasional drop shot is demoralising and tiring for opponents, making them run up to the net to cover it. Try using underspin as this causes the ball to take a flatter trajectory and to bounce lower making your opponent run further.

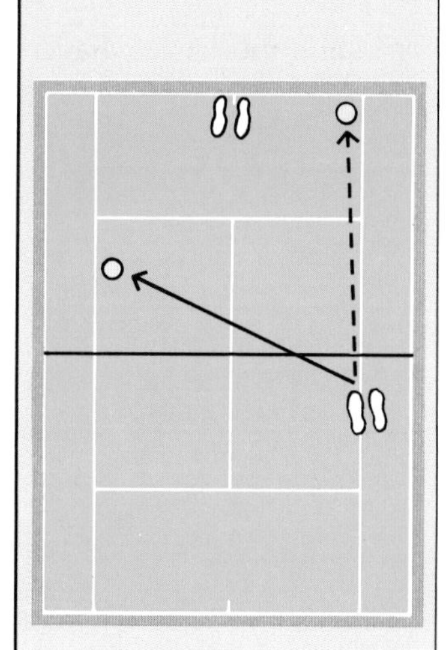

When forced wide by an opponent at the baseline try for a cross-court winner. Even more subtle is to feint a cross-court shot and then, if your opponent starts to move to cover it, to play the ball down the line.

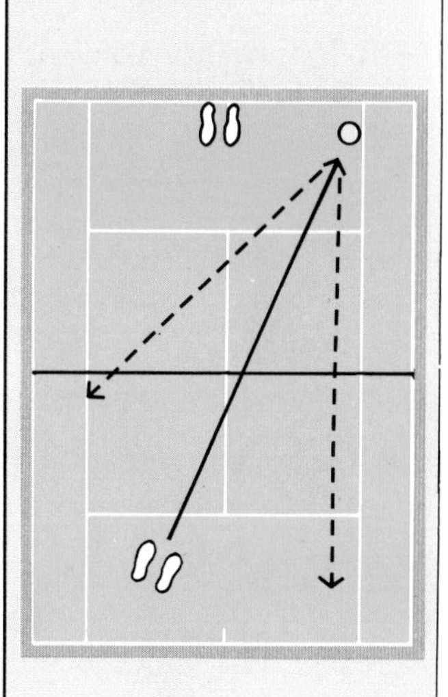

Many beginners find it tempting to return the ball to an opponent. This is because they represent a target. Try and think about space and angles when returning. Play the ball hard and deep and anticipate possible returns.

Net play

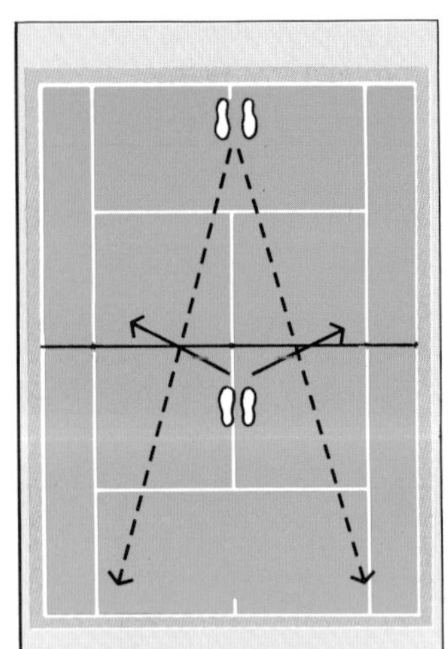

If your opponent plays a poor length ball return it deep down the centre to keep your opponent at the baseline and come forward to the net. Keep your legs apart so you can go either way. do not try to hit the ball on the run forward. By doing this you close down the angles available to the opponent and greatly increase the angles open to yourself. At the net, however, you will need to volley the ball and to react faster.

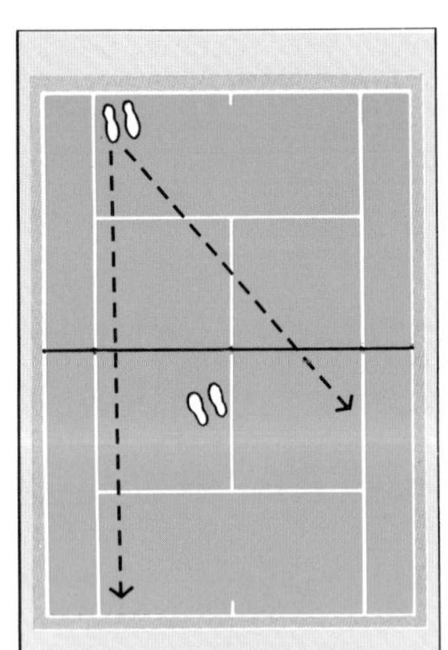

If your opponent is wide while you are at the net, remember the possible angles of return and cover accordingly. Don't go too far to cover the down-the-line shot or you will invite a cross-court return. Remember too, you can be lobbed in your present position, so keep your volleys deep and be ready to run back.

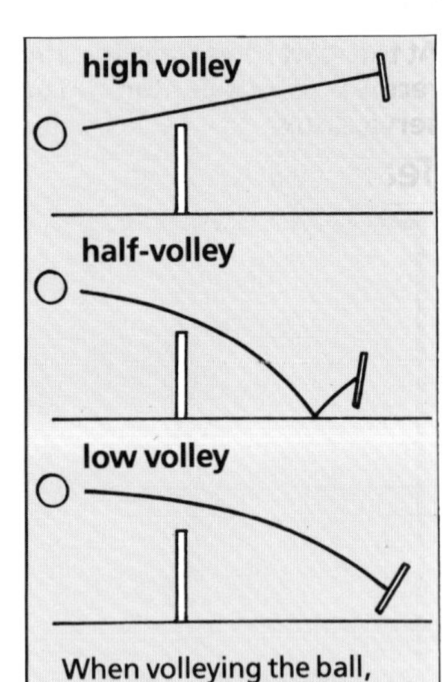

When volleying the ball, do not come too close to the net. A distance of five feet should normally be the limit. Do not backswing when volleying – the pace of the ball should be enough. You should only have to obstruct the ball's path with the firmly-held racket.
Consider, too, the half-volley. Taking the ball just after the bounce can be more effective than scraping for a low-volley. A difficult shot however, requiring perfect timing and balance.

Doubles Tactics

At the start of each point, the server's partner should be positioned at the net. The receiver stands behind the baseline and the receiver's partner stands just inside the service box.

Team work

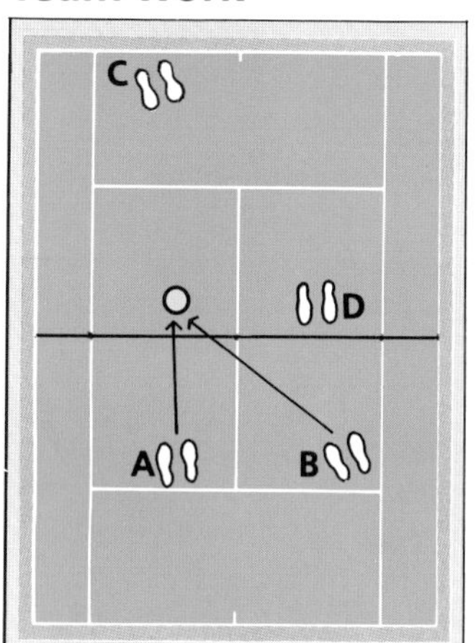

Once the rally begins, both players should play forward or both players should play back.

If one player is positioned forward and one back during a rally, as above, then both players are out of position for the drop shot on the left or for the cross-court volley.

It is vital to communicate during the game and to agree any strategies beforehand.

Poaching

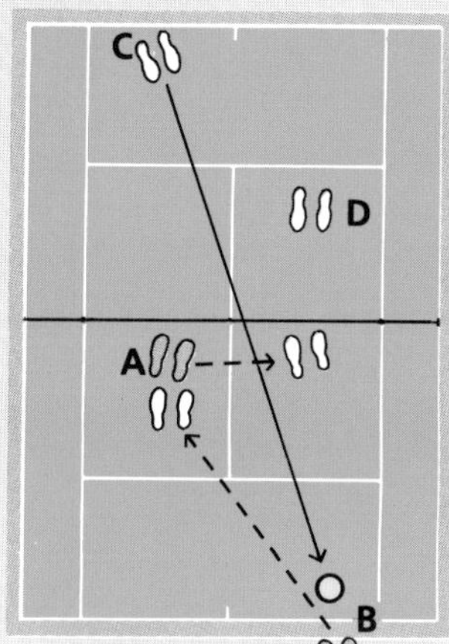

Assume player B is serving from the right-hand court. If player A moves to intercept the ball at the net then player B should move up to take A's original position on the left – player A should then continue over to the right. Again this requires communication. Call 'mine' to alert your partner of your intentions.

Lobs

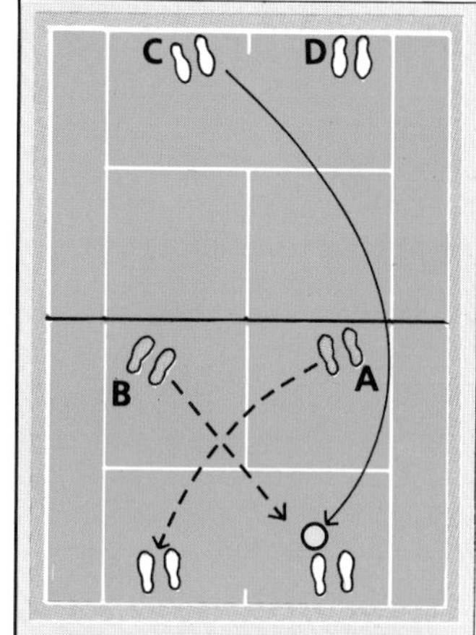

If both players are playing at the net and they are lobbed then both players should move back to avoid a front-and-back arrangement.

Players can either take lobs on their own side or on their partner's side. If the latter occurs then the lob retriever must call 'mine', partners then change sides and retreat temporarily to the back of the court. Lobs sent down the middle should always be taken by the partner with the best smash.

Bad Habits

After playing for a few months most players tend to get into bad habits. Here are four of the most common mistakes made.

No man's land

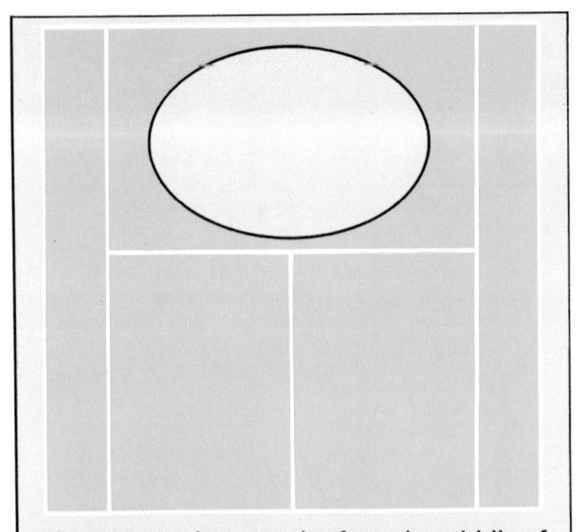

There is a tendency to play from the middle of the court or 'no man's land'. A player positioned here has none of the advantages of net play nor of the extra time gained from playing at the back.

Learn to stay well back until you can choose the correct moment to come up to the net. Play a good length ball from the back and then come forward quickly to within 5ft (1.52m) of the net. You may well lose points to begin with but the benefits will soon become apparent as you become more adventurous and your attacking play improves.

One grip

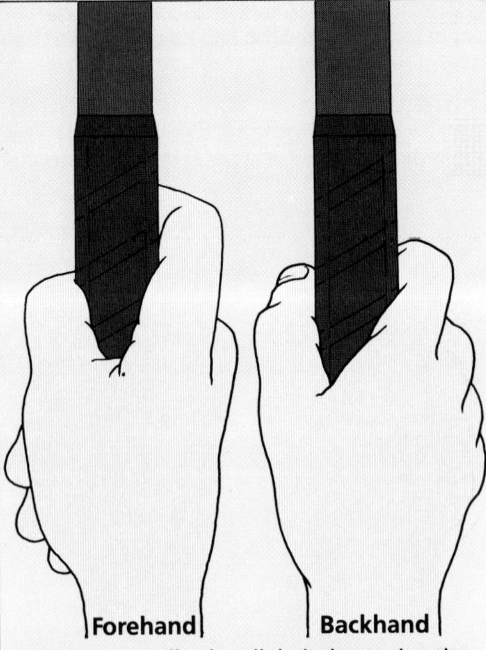

Beginners usually play all their shots using the forehand grip. This will seriously limit your game.

To improve your serve you should adopt the chopper grip – a powerful grip halfway between the forehand and the backhand grips (see page 23).

Very few can play a good backhand without changing to a one- or two-handed backhand grip (see page 23). This requires practice and determination but if you don't adopt the correct grip you will find it very hard to improve your game.

Running round the backhand

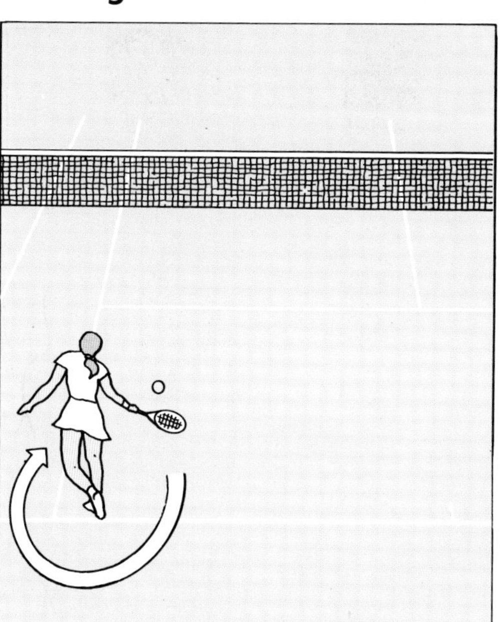

Most beginners find the backhand shot difficult. This is partly because they don't change grips and partly because the shot doesn't come as naturally as the forehand. To avoid playing the backhand, beginners often run round the shot to play it on the forehand. This is an extremely bad habit firstly because if the backhand is not practised it will never improve and secondly because it leads to terrible positioning.

Not calling

In doubles one of the worst faults is lack of communication. One player may go forward unexpectedly with no regard for their partner left stranded at the back. Or, at the net, both players may go for the same shot and clash rackets. Another common mistake is for neither partner to go for a lob, or for both players to end up on the same side of the court trying to retrieve the lobbed ball.

Good communication between partners both on and off court can prevent such situations from arising.

Glossary

ADVANTAGE After reaching deuce the next point to be won is known as an advantage (*see* page 14).

BACKSPIN This slows the ball in flight and causes a lower, slower bounce. Achieved using a chopping action under the ball. Also called UNDERSPIN.

BASELINE The line furthest from the net.

CENTRE LINE The line dividing the left and right service courts.

CHOPPER GRIP *see* CONTINENTAL GRIP.

CONTINENTAL GRIP The grip, in between the forehand and the backhand, used by more advanced players for serving and volleying. Also known as the CHOPPER GRIP (*see* page 23).

DEUCE If the score is 40-40 it is described as deuce (*see* page 14).

DOUBLE FAULT Two consecutive serving faults resulting in the server losing a point.

DRIVE A shot played just below waist height in which the ball is driven as low as possible over the net, deep into the opponent's court.

DROP SHOT A shot hit so lightly that it just drops onto the court on the other side of the net. Often hit with spin and/or disguised.

HALF-VOLLEY A return where the ball is struck immediately after it has bounced.

LET Usually describes a service where the ball has hit the net but still gone into the correct service court. To 'play a let' means to play that point again.

LOB A return hit high enough to pass over an opponent's upstretched racket forcing the opponent to the rear court.

NET CORD The name given to a ball which hits the net on its way over. A let is played if this occurs during service only.

POINT A rally, the result of which is scored.

RALLY The period during which the ball is in play.

SERVICE LINE The line parallel to the net delimiting the area within which the ball must bounce during service.

SIDESPIN Usually imparted during the service. The ball is 'sliced' with the racket to spin sideways. The ball veers slightly in the direction of spin in flight and significantly after the bounce.

SLICE Any shot played with a lot of sidespin.

SMASH A stroke, similar to the service, in which a high ball is returned at a steep angle by hitting downwards with maximum force.

STOP VOLLEY A volley where the racket absorbs some or all of the velocity of the ball.

TIE-BREAK In most tournaments, and at the discretion of recreational players, if the score reaches 6-6 a tie-break is played to settle the set. Usually not played in the final set (*see* page 15).

TOPSPIN A forward spin where the ball dips in flight and then bounces higher, achieved by stroking the racket up the back of the ball as it is hit.

TRAMLINES The name given to the parallel lines running down both sides of the tennis court. The outer is the boundary of the doubles court, the inner the boundary of the singles court (*see* page 7).

UNDERSPIN *see* BACKSPIN.

VOLLEY A return where the ball is struck before it bounces.